## LEGENDARY GREEK NAMES

# PROMETHEUS
## AND PANDORA'S BOX

JILL DUDLEY

PUT IT IN YOUR POCKET SERIES
ORPINGTON PUBLISHERS

*Published by*
Orpington Publishers

*Cover design and origination by*
Creeds, Bridport, Dorset
01308 423411

*Printed and bound in the UK by*
Creeds

© Jill Dudley 2023

ISBN: 978-0-9955781-7-3

# PROMETHEUS

## AND PANDORA'S BOX

The grandparents of Prometheus were Gaea (Mother Earth) and Ouranos (the Heavens). Gaea was self-conceived out of Chaos and then gave birth to Ouranos; together they produced the race of immortal Titans from whom eventually the gods were born. Prometheus himself was the son of the Titan Iapetus and the Titaness Themis (the personification of Justice).

Later, under the rule of the gods, according to ancient sources, Prometheus (whose name means 'forethought') fashioned Man out of clay. This greatly angered Zeus, supreme god of the twelve Olympian gods, as he had also been about to create Man. He therefore quickly found fault with those moulded by Prometheus who had already annoyed Zeus in another matter. He had once shown Zeus two parcels of meat: one of succulent fat which he had craftily wrapped around an ox's entrails, and the other of its best cuts of beef well concealed within its stomach. Lord Zeus, confident that he knew all things, failed on this occasion to detect this trickery and chose the fat-covered entrails. From then on, whenever men sacrificed to the gods, they benefited because they feasted on the best joints of beef. Every sacrificial event consequently became a communal banquet and celebration.

For these two misdemeanours Zeus, who at that time was a despot and gloried in his power, withdrew fire from men, thus depriving them of heat and light and the wherewithal to work with metal – these nonentities of human beings needed to know who ruled the heavens and the earth!

Prometheus, however, was on the side of mankind and managed to steal a little fire from Hephaestus, god of fire and metal-work. This he placed in the hollow stalk of a fennel plant and carried it back down to earth. When Lord Zeus that night saw men with their myriad lights, he was enraged and commanded his son Hephaestus to clamp iron manacles on Prometheus' wrists and ankles and pinion him to a rock in the Caucasus. To compound the torment, an eagle was sent to attack Prometheus. Daily it hovered before the unhappy captive, beating its great wings, while it clawed and pecked at his liver. Although by day the eagle tore at it with its talons and devoured it, every night it grew back again because Prometheus was a Titan and immortal.

Prometheus, however, held secret information concerning Zeus which he declared he would not reveal unless Zeus was prepared to set him free. Anxious to know what the secret was, Zeus eventually allowed his hero son, the great Heracles*, to shoot the eagle and release Prometheus.

Once freed, Prometheus informed Zeus that if either he or his brother Poseidon, god of the sea, married Thetis, a semi-divine sea-nymph, of whom both Zeus and Poseidon were enamoured, he knew it was ordained that any son born to Thetis would become greater than the father. Any danger of that sort undermining his supremacy caused Zeus hastily to see that Thetis married King Peleus of Phthia. It was, in fact, their wedding that was to trigger the Trojan War in which their son Achilles* won glory and renown and became, as predicted, greater than his father Peleus.

Because Heracles set him free from his chains, Prometheus gave him help with his eleventh Labour by telling him how to succeed in stealing the golden apples of the Hesperides – the Hesperides were the daughters of Atlas. The apples of the Hesperides were guarded by Ladon, a monstrous dragon with a hundred heads. This Labour must have seemed a daunting one for the great hero. However, with the help of Prometheus, he succeeded. First, Prometheus told Heracles to go to Atlas, who himself had been condemned for eternity to hold up the heavens on his shoulders. He was to offer to relieve him of the burden on condition he fetch the golden apples for him. Atlas, glad to be relieved of his heavy load, readily agreed. Taking over the weight of the heavens, Heracles waited for Atlas to return. When he arrived, however, Atlas refused to hold up the heavens again, and Heracles had to resort to trickery. He asked Atlas to take the heavens for a brief moment while he padded his shoulders because they were becoming chafed under the weight. When Atlas supported the heavens again, Heracles quickly gathered up the golden apples and disappeared.

Ever vengeful because of Prometheus' help to mankind, Zeus decided to cause men untold trouble by creating a woman, and he commanded his son Hephaestus to do this for him. The name given to this first woman was Pandora (meaning 'all gifts'). The goddess Athena breathed life into her, gave her beauty and dressed her in fine clothes; while Hermes (another son of Zeus) taught her guile.

This first woman was given as a bride to Prometheus' brother Epimetheus (his name means 'after-thought' or 'hindsight') – in other words he acted first and thought afterwards. Along with his new bride Epimetheus received a sealed box which he was ordered never to open.

Prometheus with his forethought was aware of the danger of this beautiful woman, and he warned his brother not to accept any gift from the gods. But Epimetheus was very happy with his lovely new bride, and had no intention of rejecting the gift that came with her.

Being a woman (and all ills from then on were blamed on women) Pandora was seized with curiosity regarding her mysterious box. Did it contain jewellery, or spices, or gold? It was irresistable, and one day she just had to know what was inside. She lifted the lid a fraction and wham! Out flew all the evils of the world – sins, diseases, anxieties, humours, tempers and everything that was to become a perpetual plague to men. Pandora quickly slammed down the lid, but not before the sins had escaped miraculously leaving Hope trapped inside. And so it was that when things looked at their bleakest, Hope was always there to give encouragement. A parallel could be drawn with the Old Testament story of Adam and Eve where all the sins of the world was the fault of Eve for being unable to resist temptation by eating the fruit of the tree of knowledge.

Pandora and Epimetheus had a daughter whom they called Pyrrha. When she grew up she married Deucalion, a son of Prometheus. By now the sins of the world had got such a grip on human beings that Zeus decided to send a flood and destroy the lot of them. It was Prometheus, thanks to his foresight, who warned his son Deucalion to build a boat and take on board a store of food – again a story similar to the Old Testament one of Noah's ark.

Deucalion and his wife were afloat for nine days before Zeus called a halt to the deluge. After that the floods began to abate: Deucalion's ark eventually came to rest on Mt. Parnassus, close to the Delphic oracle where at the time their forebear, the earth-goddess Gaia (Mother Earth) had her sanctuary.

When Deucalion and Pyrrha realized they were the only survivors of the flood, they longed for fellow human beings and beseeched the gods not to leave them totally bereft of their own kind. Either Zeus' son Hermes or, as some said, it was the Delphic oracle itself, Deucalion and his wife were told to throw the bones of their mother over their shoulders to produce a new crop of humans.

To disturb the bones of the dead they knew would be a sacrilegious act; but in time it dawned on them that the oracle must have been referring to the stones from the ground since their forebear was Gaia. They therefore threw stones from the ground. To their joy those thrown by Deucalion sprang up as men, and those by Pyrrha became women. And so a new race of humankind was born.

So what became of Prometheus? Well, as an immortal Titan he was destined to live for ever. His was a strange story because he dared defy the supreme unyielding and ruthless god of the heavens whose power was absolute. It was thanks to Prometheus that mankind won a measure of freedom, and his gift of fire was invaluable because it gave men the ability to progress in life. As for the despot Zeus, he learned that to show compassion was better than using brute force and tyranny.

When Christianity spread amongst the pagans, the story of Prometheus was used as an example to win over the pagan mind to Christ who too was a Saviour who suffered for mankind.

*\* Denotes a separate booklet on the subject.*

# GLOSSARY

ACHILLES – Greek hero of the Trojan War, son of King Peleus and Thetis.

ATHENA – Daughter of Zeus and Metis. Athena was goddess of handicraft and protectress of Athens. Her symbol was the owl, and she was the embodiment of wisdom.

ATLAS – Son of Iapetus (a Titan) and Clymene, a daughter of Oceanus. As punishment for his part in the revolt of the Titans against the gods, he was compelled to support the heavens on his shoulders for all time.

DEUCALION – Son of Prometheus and an ocean nymph. His wife was his cousin Pyrrha.

EPIMETHEUS – Brother of Prometheus, married to Pandora. His name means 'after-thought'.

GAIA – The personification of the earth (Mother Earth).

HEPHAESTUS – Lame son of Zeus and Hera. He was god of fire and metal-craft.

HERA – Wife and sister of Zeus, mother of Hephaestus, Hebe and Ares.

HERACLES – Son of Zeus and a mortal woman Alcmena (wife of King Amphitryon of Tiryns). He was noted for his strength and courage, and his Twelve Labours. The Romans knew him as Hercules.

HERMES – Messenger son of Zeus and the mortal beauty Maia. He also conducted the souls of the dead down to Hades.

HESPERIDES – Daughters of Atlas. There were four or seven in number, and lived in the far West where they guarded an apple tree that produced golden apples. The tree was guarded by the ever watchful serpent Ladon who had a hundred heads.

IAPETUS – Father of Atlas, Prometheus and Epimetheus by Clymene.

METIS – Mother of Athena by Zeus. Her name means 'counsel'.

OURANOS – The personification of the heavens, who married Gaea (Mother Earth). They became grand-parents to many Olympian gods.

PANDORA – The first woman created by Zeus and sent to be a pest to the first man who was created by Prometheus. She married Epimetheus and was responsible for the sins of the world by opening the sealed box that came with him which she had been warned never to open.

PELEUS – King of Phthia. He married Thetis and their son was Achilles.

POSEIDON – Brother of Zeus. He was god of the sea, horses and earthquakes.

PYRRHA – Daughter of Epimetheus and Pandora. She married Deucalion.

THETIS – A semi-divine sea-nymph who married King Peleus. Their son was Achilles.

TITANS – Pre-Olympian gods or demi-gods, the offspring of Ouranos and Gaea.

ZEUS – Supreme god of the twelve Olympians. He was married to Hera but had numerous extra-marital affairs with mortal beauties by whom he fathered children.

MORE FROM THE PUT IT IN YOUR POCKET SERIES:

## GREEK MYTHS
THE JUDGEMENT OF PARIS
HELEN
KING AGAMEMNON
ACHILLES
THE WOODEN HORSE
ODYSSEUS

## ISLANDS
CHIOS – HOMER
CRETE – THESEUS AND THE MINOTAUR
DELOS – BIRTHPLACE OF APOLLO
ITHAKA – ODYSSEUS
KOS – HIPPOCRATES AND ASCLEPIUS
LESBOS (MYTILENE) – SAPPHO AND ORPHEUS
NAXOS – THESEUS AND THE MINOTAUR
PATMOS – ST. JOHN THE THEOLOGIAN
RHODES – THE COLOSSUS
SAMOS – PYTHAGORAS AND THE HERAION
SANTORINI – THE LOST ISLAND OF ATLANTIS
TINOS – THE MIRACLE-WORKING ICON

## SACRED SITES
ATHENS – THE ACROPOLIS
ELEUSIS – DEMETER AND KORE
EPIDAURUS – CENTRE OF HEALING
DELPHI – THE ORACLE OF APOLLO
CORINTH – ST. PAUL AND THE GODDESS OF LOVE
OLYMPIA – THE OLYMPIC GAMES

ALSO BY JILL DUDLEY:

YE GODS!
(TRAVELS IN GREECE)

YE GODS! II
(MORE TRAVELS IN GREECE)

HOLY SMOKE!
(TRAVELS IN TURKEY AND EGYPT)

GODS IN BRITAIN
(AN ISLAND ODYSSEY FROM PAGAN TO CHRISTIAN)

MORTALS AND IMMORTALS
(A SATIRICAL FANTASY & TRUE-IN-PARTS MEMOIR)

HOLY FIRE!
(TRAVELS IN THE HOLY LAND)

LAP OF THE GODS
(TRAVELS IN CRETE AND THE AEGEAN ISLANDS)

GODS & HEROES
(ON THE TRAIL OF THE ILIAD & THE ODYSSEY)

BEHIND THE MASKS
(IN THE FOOTSTEPS OF THE EARLY GREEK DRAMATISTS)

OH, SOCRATES!
(TRACKING THE LIFE AND DEATH OF SOCRATES)